Color of Her Speech

Color of Her Speech

Lola Lemire Tostevin

THE COACH HOUSE PRESS, TORONTO

Copyright © Lola Lemire Tostevin, 1982

Published with the assistance of the Canada Council and the Ontario Arts Council.

ISBN 0-88910-255-4

Even as a melody is not composed of tones, nor a verse of words, nor a statue of lines, one must pull and tear a unity into a multiplicity, so it is with the human being to whom I say You. I can abstract from him the color of his hair or the color of his speech or the color of his graciousness; I have to do this again and again; but immediately he is no longer You.
MARTIN BUBER

but mom
speaking both
french and english
is like having two watches

you're never sure
what time it is
PETER

◇

*tout ce qui commence
par amour
se divise
se multiplie*

en singularités

*le seing des reins
se compose
pour se décomposer*

*dénomme
pour dénoncer*

*mais jamais
on se défait
de nos cicatrices
Majuscules*

◇

4 words french
1 word english

slow seepage
slow seepage

3 words french
2 words english

rattling off
or running at the mouth

2 words french
3 words english

speak white

or as Buber writes
you have abstracted from me
the color of my hair
the color of my speech

1 word french
4 words english

'tu déparles'
my mother says

je déparle
        yes

I unspeak

◇

the Unspeaking
the Unbinding of Umbilicals
ba be bi bo
'déparler'
décomposer
sa langue
da de di do

'*l'enfant do*
l'enfant dormira bien vite'

'and if that lullaby don't sing
 papa's gonna buy you a diamond
 ring ..!'

la source renversée
the course unlaid

baby lulled
by a lie

byaliebyaliebyaliebyaliebyalie

◇

the dream is french
present past unbroken
what's lost lasts

> *une enfant parcourt une encyclopédie
> et tombe sur des machines à mesurer
> le temps ... sabliers cadrans poètes ...*

awake
each moment translates
like a clock
          measures
the present
angle of vision
temps
      into time
tic
   into toc

head rhyme
tic toc

an atomic alliteration
an-atomic-al

slow invagination
of the temporal bone

◇

'french is no longer
my mother tongue' she says

'neither is english' he says

'well what is'

'fucking' he says

so when people inquired
as to her first language
she replied 'fuckinese'

'about poetry
keep it nameless' he says
'an author is inconsequential
to a good piece of art'

tongueless fucking in the dark

taking the light
the naming

two missing measures

time

◇

where
and with what words
do we begin?

from the beginning
there were two words
always
one word then another

twice removed

two cries
breaking the face
                the stone

two silences

comment tu t'appelles?
what is your name?

comment tu t'appelles?
what is your name?

defective c(h)ord
caught on a nail
splitting the air

until two
(like the eyes)
is felt as one

and one
becomes one
             half

◇

> la victime n'est pas celui ou celle
> qui subit mais celui ou celle qui
> tient un certain langage
> ROLAND BARTHES

call it what you will
defection
fetish
but please understand
it was never a case
of clear choice

fascist little carriers
pushing just below the surface
invading the unclear spaces
all that ifness
fantasy
love
forever and ever
or as Richard said
those words he avoids like the plague

remember the game?
would you sooner be
a man or a woman
french or english
and if you absolutely absolutely had to choose
would you be blind
or deaf and dumb

nazi or jew?

given this
or that difference
as opposition
I would have chosen
Purity
The Sense-less
The Anti-Body
instead of

how do you say it
in your language
and will it ease
the queasy longing?

◇

it isn't that
the faded voice betrayed
its speaker

it's just that it failed
to get an answer

that is the story of evolution

chameleon thinking grey white
in dark cool places
thinks absence
thinks extinction
subjugates to conjugate
a guise
her body a white lie
bloodless
in the blankness
              of that space

'and where is your colorful accent'
they all ask
so white
so black
seeking a difference
they can touch and taste

   accent aigu
   accent grave
   accent circonflexe

stress
       small hook
in the flesh

you could say
she comes to you bearing
false witness

telling it
as it is

◇

*vide s'accroche
à sa bouche
se remplit
de battement d'ailes*

*ventre plein
de frémissements*

*une langue
qui abandonne son nid
ne goutte plus*

aux oiseaux

◇

to remove the whole
of the tongue the mouth
is widely opened
with a gag the organ
transfixed with silk

the glossus divided
with a pair of scissors
écraseurs or crushers
the base cut through
by a series of short snips

as it becomes easier
to pull the tongue
well out of the mouth
each vessel is dealt with
as soon as divided
the remaining undivided
portion of the organ
seized with forceps
and lifted from the cavity

in cases where only one side
of the tongue
needs to be eliminated
the operation is modified
by splitting the tongue
down the centre
the affected half removed
through the neck
through a semilunar incision
along the lower jaw
extending backward to the hyoid bone

the tongue can then be reached
through the floor of the mouth
and removed with the crushers

the main objection to this operation
is that the larynx
and all the muscles in the area
are divided
preventing normal breathing

once
the mouth
stood empty

it was easy
to introduce
your difference

◇

*langue étrangère
efface les traces
des contes enfantins*

*scelle la mer
de nos bateaux à voiles*

*ce qui se définit
devient inexprimable*

*la plume
un glaçon par quoi`
le poème se décompose*

*la page
l'envers d'une neige
qui coule et disparait*

*le corps se défile
pour laisser un blanc*

*arrive à sa fin
sans commencement*

◇

which part
of the body
speaks (or the sensation of
)
which beat
which breath yields the form by
which

it all comes about

we said: the body
is a poem
of coordinated parts

we said: one
is so dependent
upon the other so united
we can speak now
of penetration

we said: language
is opposed
to all that

listen to us eye
to eye too
close to catch

you said: let's see
how deep down your throat I can thrust

it stopped
there

it takes
a different tongue
to penetrate
a different depth

◇

mother
        tongue
memory
        drawing
towards with —

drawing

        retracing
        retrieving

à la source
à la dérive

adrift

driving along the shore
of the St Lawrence
on a sunny March morning
babbling french with Jean Marcel
after all these years

river
        frozen
              fixed

fleuve
flows back

to *vague*
memory

◇

chuchoter...

soft sound
between you

        and I

'this is why
the element of speech
is air..!

but air
is not my element

I am not in my element

so when you say
you cannot hear
as if there were
two voices

        two sounds pulled
by the current
of lost breath

when
the still small voice
                goes under

trails
      into a whisper
               through fear

of a separate pulse

draw near
your ear
against my mouth
and catch
        my breath

◇

and you leaving
in a few days
for clear colors

and stories

so little to be seen
here

light snow
burning logs
detachment
all dissolving settings

and The Silent Treatment
old syntax to articulate
what can't be shaped

what can no longer be held

you watched my hand stroking the dog
recorded my hand moving mechanically
over the dog's back
and I recorded your recording
the only one enjoying the moment
being the blissfully stupid dog

you left
my hand
in your eye
stony
in your bony
orbit

◇

of course we didn't mean
those things
we said

expression
so often unrelated
to meaning

and of course
we didn't mean the way
we acted

meaning
so often unrelated
to action

so whatever love is
it is not
what we said
how we acted

but tell me
        if you can

what
was the intention

◇

4 am

all night
all we've done is talk
about them
husbands
lovers
and all the others lurking
between

all night
and yesterday
and the day before

300 convent girls mouthing
Credos
Pater Nosters
to an Invisible
Omnipotent Peeping Tom

another night of Cravens As
too much Courvoisier
hangover already pressing
behind the sockets

tomorrow
another day unable to forget
this goddamned ritual

as the red & yellow Mr. Donut neon
revolves and hits my window

our words appear
disappear

forever

◇

he writes
we risked
a music
together

that was no risk

we marked
a space
and with it's
passing

each touch
each sound
awakened
this song

baby baby been on this road
so many times
no longer have to
read the signs

◇

> In Sanskrit, kedesha, independent woman
> is a synonym for harlot....
> ERICH NEUMAN
> *The Origins and History of Consciousness*

Blanche Neige
La Belle au Bois Dormant

language disappears
still repeats itself

woman written
woman dreamed
kedesha holy
kedesha whore

The Undifferentiated Function
French Freud Sanskrit
myths and legends
as old as men

and oh how you love women
who are sealed
seek women
who are nameless
for nothing quickens
your imagination
as a siren without repertory

Hérodiade
La Belle Dame Sans Merci
The Lady of Shalott
breathed into animation

kedesha kedesha

and now that you are looking
for another woman
who are you leaving?

kedesha?

kedesha

◇

standing in line
at the International Cinema
a passerby asks
'what's playing'

uncertain how to translate
Sauve Qui Peut (La Vie)
which I find later is
Every Man for Himself
I just say 'something by Godard'

stranger muttering
'Jesus you don't even know
the name of the film'

◇

it's clear
after all the reading
mankind speaks
but one language

differences skin deep
reach
one anchored depth

one underlying flow
which to all men is the same

it's clear
after all the reading
they've all overlooked

the monad deme

can be a nomad
and a dame

◇

at minus 40° it's a no man's land
no woman's either
few signs of life

except for fly wheel ravens
mute black vanes
tracing cataracts so thick
it's night by 4 o'clock
time to mourn the loss
of some imagined place

in an obvious attempt to help crush the silence
the children combine
coloring books
fat iridescent crayons
french lessons

fill space
name shapes
body of things

   tête ronde et rose
   oeil jaune
   bouche rouge en coeur

the mouth a valentine
heart
       of this alien condition

   bras bleus verts mauves
   corps multicolores

fingers tight and careful
not to wander
on both sides

of the fine lines

◇

what tames
the defiance
of things no longer
here nor there

   silence golden
   love red
   moods dark

what colors the air?

on my desk
facing the large front window
which traps everything
on either side
the prism I use as paperweight
has caught the light
bent it
into new positions

The body has been made so problematic for women that it has often seemed easier to shrug it off and travel as a disembodied spirit.

...we must touch the unity and resonance of our physicality, our bond with the natural order, the corporeal ground of our intelligence.

ADRIENNE RICH

...it is through colors that the subject escapes its alienation within a code.

JULIA KRISTEVA

◇

Time Magazine art critic Robert Hughes
reviewing Judy Chicago's The Dinner Party
sculpture dedicated to women of history
calls it 'static ... cliché ... hokey ...
obsessive stereotype ... mass devotional ...
colors worthy of a Taiwanese souvenir factory ...
evangelical ... free of wit or irony ..!
then goes on to label Chicago's explanation
for choosing the vagina as her mark
of otherness and identity
as 'jargon'
and 'femspeak'

few months later Hughes tells the Globe and Mail
his favorite art form has always been surrealism
his favorite artist Joan Miró because
'it's adolescent youth-culture stuff ...
and like a baby duck you fixate
on the first thing you see
and that's mom ..!

of course
and mom doesn't have a cunt
especially if she's male surrealist
whose work has been described
as 'emblematic ... biomorphic abstraction ...
amorphous shapes floating in ambiguous space ..!

menspeak?

femspeak
jargon
gutteral voiceless
sound
      slang
            language
originating with
nomads
thieves
whores
gypsies

in Quebec we say
argot
argoter to cut
a dead branch
the semantic cut
            cunt

woman's cant
        rant
            rent

breach deep
and wide
      femspeak
woman's span

◇

in light
(of speech?)

still life
stirs
    the eye
    the sun

conceived
as white assumes
its yellow tinge
and black to blue

horizon / orison

on the lip
on the tip
of tongue –

        shaped clit –

oris ora oriflamme
red as silky after-birth

her mouth
her sex

shape of breath
and origanum

Gyno-Text

for Lisa

Out of O
into
the
narrow
bare
but
for
this
foreign
marrow

oral
pit
spits
yolk
spins
spine

embryo
rolls
like
a
scroll

breath
of
bone
by
bone
body's
first
articulation
arteriole
first
vowel

voice
boxed
in
ears
echo
deeper
pounding
tympa
tym
     panic
rhythm
of a
heart
some
w]here

eye
ball O
n stalk
sucks
brain
flows
Over
lid
fOld

opened
furrOw
shows
its
sex
translated
palate
joined
as
one

taste
bud
trickles
salt
in
fine
hair
filament

heart
hollow
dividing
two
ounces
of
bloody
love
and
bitter
ness

brain
bloom
white
web
hemmed
in
spheres
hung
loose
ly

mute
skeleton
moves
to
muscle
string
pulled
taut
from
A
to
Zone

vagin
vagir
enfin

◇

for Peter

why is it
every second or third day
the old archetypes move into our kitchen
sit at our table
squabble over curfews
allowance money
hockey rules ...

Mother Dragon breathing fire
upon the young hero
who stands unflinching
erect before the morning monster
the devouring maw
chained to the crag
grown fast to the rock
until finally young Samson slams doors
threatening pillars on the entire block
probably out to rescue
some young maiden
while the slain and vengeful Fury
fumes over a fourth cup of coffee ...

last night at a poetry reading
a poet read how as a young boy
his mother threatened
to send him to an asylum
the scandalized audience
shaking its head in disbelief

my beautiful blond son
at 6'3" &
with your direct line to God
how can I not look up to you

in spite of all the lunatics
raging through our kitchen
paving the way   I swear
there is no going back
never to the point
where it's either you
or I

◇

those places dis
continuous
where weight of words
no longer measures
distances

and the last tear
is parched and dry
as bone

they are
not limits

changes
changeless
change again

as past tense
moves the mood
to present's
small conjunction as

unless   except   until

all turn
to coincide
around sharp corners

other matters
of fact

◇

the loss of a limb

withdrawal of a sense
they say
sharpens all others

old deaf woman
squatting on the sidewalk
drones a sound that sounds

in her ears
and mine

and the noise
when that man pounds
the hospital corridors

is in his missing leg

the amputated
truncated text
follows an imaginary line

and grows
extravagant

if not to the things themselves
a trace

art
in the artificial glass eye

thesis
in prosthesis

none
less real

◇

round and round
where love is blind
and having to speak
the same language

not mine

converse reverse
conserve reserve
the contradiction

   à contre-temps
   à contre-coeur

the subject not subject
to change the better
takes another turn
for the worse
vicious circle's limit
leaves nothing behind or
to the imagination

there's the angle ...
a difference
which doesn't yet exist

nothing
between you and I

between the abstraction
and all the badinage

nothing to hold us
together
holds us apart

◇

grafted tongue
is the seeing eye
now

tearing into hybrid birds
who barely linger
there

wags and guides
its own keen sense
towards the pitch
dark

trans / parent

to speak the look-out
for the other half

truth
       and double cross

to bear
the telling
of what it feels

I always knew

◇

in this age of Transcendence
patterns as old as original sins
will not be transcended ...

instinct? stint for life?
when body taps reason
then each goes its separate way?

when a poet's turn of head
obliterates
his turn of phrase

or the instructor's tights
set you dreaming during a strenuous
class of stretch and strength

even the hairdresser whom you know sings
Italian love songs to all his customers
and for whom you feel only contempt
and anger
              and a sudden fleet of gondolas
rushing along the neural canals
the pelvic basin
              visceral arch

head screaming
steady steady
my rudimentary

heart

◇

makes one wonder where
all this leads
a middle age   middle class
housewife

   pots
   pans
   gnosis

no household word
this food for thought

meat   blood simmering
on the back burner
while the fridge purrs
like a blank page
an empty belly

these
could be colors or contours
against the void
but there's little room
for madness here
or romanticism

some days this small asylum shreds
and assimilates well

there is cognitition in the Cuisinart

'and don't ever trust anyone
who doesn't understand the basics
of preparing food'
she advises her family
a house guest she knows can't cook
worth a damn

'they lack a common knowledge'

smirk and carves the meat the way
she yearns to slice through

with a sharp
and merciless
edge

◇

so many days
when it is still
a question of detachment

on one hand
desire
on the other

whose shape
to choose out of whose
desire?

mother lover poet
'upon a body made to offer
every bliss appears two heads'

or three

on a postcard from Australia this morning
there is the back of a Samoan
so thoroughly tattooed
at first I thought he was wearing pyjamas

the message reads 'well it is different
from masks I suppose'

the beginning then
nakedness so conspicuous
so censored it shrieked

out of context

carved flesh
changes the fiction

and the body
now that it is a body
can be rightfully read

and must we
only
read it?

◇

3 pm

put down The Origin of the Work of Art
which I don't understand
turn on 5 minutes of soap
One Life to Live
which I don't understand

my head another area
always caught in between

sit down to write
for the book
which makes visible
something other
than itself

unconceals

      implicates

between two

which fails
if one is false
the other true

mouth twisting
the arm to form

a poem

between

the way I speak
the way I spoke

Special thanks to Barrie Nichol for his encouragement,
editing, and for being the first one to tell me that
I could. Also to Grant Goodbrand for being the
first one to say that I should.

Seen through the Press by bpNichol
Cover design by Gordon Robertson
Typeset in Trump and printed in Canada. 72 pp.

For a list of other books you might enjoy,
write for our catalogue of books in print,
or call us at (416) 979-2217.

THE COACH HOUSE PRESS
401 (rear) Huron Street
Toronto, Canada M5S 2G5